Memoirs of a Witness Tree

Memoirs of a Witness Tree

Poems by

Randal A. Burd, Jr.

Cover art by Annabel Lee Burd
Cover design by Shay Culligan

ISBN: 978-1-952326-31-8

Kelsay Books
502 South 1040 East, A-119
American Fork, Utah, 84003

To those muses who have befriended, encouraged, mentored, and otherwise made this life worth living, I dedicate this work. I have been blessed with far more than I deserve.

To my greatest blessings, Annabel and Everett.

Acknowledgments

Amethyst Review: "An Affirmation of Faith?"

Friends of the Falun Gong: "Indoctrinating Evil"

Halftime Magazine: "Reconnaissant Pour L'esprit de Corps"

Nine Muses Poetry: "Bad News," "Circus Elephants in Retirement," "Echoes of Yesterday," "Encroaching Weeds," "Physician of the Mind," "The Air Grows Cold," "We Siblings Three," "What Will Stay?"

Poetry Breakfast: "The Edge of Memory"

Rue Scribe: "Blades of Doubt," "Depression's Lies," "Humblest Apologies," "Ignorance in Love," "Prematurely Blessed," "What Makes Me Happy," "While Waiting"

Snakeskin: "Grief"

The Hypertexts: "On Better Days"

The Society of Classical Poets: "Armed with Imagination," "Artisans & Fools," "Blue Spacious Skies," "Humilitas," "Made in China," "Out of Mind," "The Captain to His Mate," "The Fall of the Fourth Estate," "The Forlorn Hope—Vicksburg 1863," "This Sycamore, a Witness Tree"

The Writers' Café Magazine: "Backwoods Town," "Lost," "Overthrown"

Vita Brevis: "A Suitcase," "Forgotten," "Reflection"

Westward Quarterly: "Chaos Abounds," "Examples Made," "My Little Man"

Contents

Humblest Apologies

Too personal a thought to be laid bare,
A naked truth now shrouded in cheap rhyme.
No less profound to stand the test of time
Than those the masters once saw fit to share.

Why should a random stranger deem to care?
Expression via sonnet is a crime—
To use such an archaic paradigm
And then expect one's talent to compare.

Consider, then, emotions found within
And surely found throughout humanity
Have meant enough to someone such as me
To risk unwanted feelings of chagrin.

And thus, with ample warning, pray begin
To reassess conventionality.

Artisans & Fools

The sparks of protest fly as hammer pounds
To make a stubborn ingot sharper steel.
In pummeling, perfection will reveal
Its shifting shape with banging clanging sounds.

This repetition lasts for several rounds;
As smithy molds, the metal does appeal
For mercy from relentless hammer's zeal;
The artisan, in answer, only frowns.

When flames are duly doused and metal cools,
The finished product's polish is applied
And, only then, the maker will decide
If labor's love was worthy of his tools.
Its quality has thus identified
The difference in artisans and fools.

Armed with Imagination

Imagination armed this youthful knight—
A plywood shield and sword of sapling wood
Created echoes in the neighborhood
Of backyard battles fought in fading light.

Envision how we must have been a sight
To see—a panorama understood
By only we who fought each chance we could
While lacking rhyme or reason for a fight.

The best of memories those days remain:
Each noble quest and faux chivalric deed.
Forever will they be accompanied
With yearning for just one last grand campaign.

We Siblings Three

Attempt to add the hours we have shared:
One hundred thousand, maybe thousands more?
Our paths conjoined for several years before
We struck out on our own and even dared
Imagine we would chase our dreams beyond
The borders of our joyful, sheltered lives.
But now we live with husband and with wives
In separate towns and rarely correspond,
Or so it seems when measured and compared
To neighborhood crusades we daily swore
Would never end. But we would soon respond
To destiny. What from those days survives?
That we still share a special sibling bond
Though kept apart by long, infrequent drives.

Overthrown

I slowly cruised our former neighborhood:
Locations once familiar now are strange.
Most houses there are worse for wear and change;
No laughter echoes from the nearby wood.

When everyone grew up and moved away,
Our plywood platforms rotted in the tree.
No Robin Hood remained to climb and see
His merry men engage in daily play.

The paths we made have long since overgrown.
Our wooden forts became the forest floor.
Adventures don't occur here anymore—
Our sacred places have been overthrown.

Reconnaissant Pour L'esprit de Corps

I still recall those days of marching bands
When bonded by a fierce esprit de corps
We stepped in time and played into the stands;
Not holding back, we left them wanting more.
They came to see each small-town halftime show
What seems to me a lifetime long ago.

What seems to me a lifetime long ago,
We'd test our skills against the other bands.
Our heads held high with such esprit de corps,
We'd send our melodies into the stands.
No marching band has ever given more
Than ours when we performed our polished show.

When we performed our polished marching show
So many times, so many years ago,
We held our own among the many bands
And rode the high of our esprit de corps.
Combined with all the cheering from the stands,
That feeling always left us wanting more.

That feeling always left us wanting more,
Returning to us during every show,
But that was such a long, long time ago,
Back in those days of school and marching bands
When teamwork brought us great esprit de corps,
Rewarding us with cheering from the stands.

But now there's no more cheering from the stands.
We all moved on in search of something more.
Some hoped we'd have a little more to show
For lives which started all those years ago
When days were filled with school and marching bands
And we were filled with much esprit de corps.

Now others share the same esprit de corps
And march in time and play into the stands.
We never see each other anymore.
Reunions pass, but many never show,
Though bound together briefly long ago
By lessons learned in school and marching bands.

Esprit de corps was why in marching bands,
We'd stand up straight, chins up, for every show
And leave them wanting more those years ago.

This Sycamore, a Witness Tree

This sycamore, a witness tree,
Stood tall in 1863
As Lincoln passed by to address
The military's late success
Against the forces brought by Lee.

It witnessed every enlistee
Succumbing to a battery
Of cannon they could not suppress,
This sycamore.

No pensioner or retiree
Observed such long past history.
But though it lives, it can't profess
Such knowledge we'd have it possess.
Oh, what we'd learn, if we could be
This sycamore!

The Forlorn Hope—Vicksburg, 1863

Back in Vicksburg, the town was surrounded
With a battle line twelve miles long.
U.S. Grant sought to conquer the city,
But the rebel defenses were strong.
An advance storming party was risky;
They could possibly lose every man.
But they must cross a ditch and climb over a wall
Just to capture the Stockade Redan.

With extreme disregard for the danger,
While exposed to a torrent of lead,
The men carried their logs and their ladders
And soon painted the path with their dead.
The one hundred and fifty brave soldiers,
All unmarried and all volunteers,
Had advanced at a run while opposing cannon
Brought fresh screams to their still-ringing ears.

So, from ten in the morning 'til darkness,
They would fight the good fight 'til they fell.
A majority there didn't make it;
The remainder survived living Hell.
The survivors were honored as heroes,
Received medals almost to a man
For extreme gallantry of the storming party
At the fight for the Stockade Redan.

Prematurely Blessed

I watched her come too fast into this world.
I heard those faint unhealthy infant cries.
And as they checked her length and weight and size,
Her little fingers 'round my finger curled.

Untimely from her mother's womb was hurled
Our premature and sickly sacred prize
Who, we would later come to realize,
Became the star 'round which our planet whirled.

Her sickliness received intensive care;
Pneumonia left her lungs and let her thrive—
So lucky and so blessed to be alive!
Our lives were changed forever then and there.

And ever since our daughter did arrive,
There's never been a day that could compare.

My Little Man

I held you in my heart before I knew
Those dimpled cheeks and beaming impish grin.
Once quite the helpless creature, then you grew
Into the little man you are. And when
You speak with a maturity unearned,
Intelligence beyond your fledgling years,
Amazing me each day with what you've learned,
Your childhood much too quickly disappears.

Soon time will take this little boy from me—
Replace this child I love now with a man.
Whatever you decide you want to be,
I hope that you will always understand:

I held you in my heart when you were small,
And time won't change my love for you at all.

Examples Made

Our lives are like a looking glass
Through which our children often see
Their futures through the veil of time
With more responsibility.

From us they gain the will to live:
Learn to endure through hardships met,
Find that it's better to forgive
And how you can't escape regret.

Our happiness is theirs to share.
Our struggles help define them too.
Our choices are examples made
Of what you should—and shouldn't—do.

We fiercely hope they will succeed,
That we have given them our best,
And fondness taints their memories
Of times before they flew the nest.

What Makes Me Happy

Their eyes stare back into my own,
Familiar features long I've known,
Just lately to appreciate
The life bestowed on them by fate,
Plus circumstances mine alone.

Idyllic aspirations blown
With every disappointment—prone
To fall far short or much too late.
Their eyes stare back.

Now looking back on how they've grown—
Strong saplings from the seeds I've sown—
As opportunities abate,
I pray my love will resonate.
Most precious gifts I helped create—
Their eyes stare back.

Lost

A long-abandoned logging road still winds
Through wooded hills, off paved, familiar ways.
There, careless motorists get lost for days
While navigating hazards of all kinds.

That I'm off-course is just a simple fact.
I blindly listened to the G-P-S,
And doing so resulted in this mess—
Lost and alone on this forsaken tract.

My compact car was never meant for this.
How soon until they locate my remains?
My legacy will be my lack of brains
And absence in the lives of those I'll miss.

Then, just before the fear sets in for good,
I find my way out of the loathsome wood.

Ignorance in Love

We're innocent—how one small gesture can
Define relationships and change life's course.
We charge ahead, choose risk, and dare remorse
To end our romance right where it began.

Imagine circumvention as a plan:
Precluding fights and failures and divorce;
By ending bad engagements at the source,
We could improve the happiness of man!

But life is not all joys devoid of pain.
Who can predict each outcome of a kiss?
What moments cherished would be lost with this?
Contingencies are hard to ascertain
As are which moments we will reminisce.
Our ignorance in love is truly bliss.

Grief

The deepest wells of grief reside next door,
Just out of sight and in the back of mind,
Abstract enough that most observers find
The time to sigh but then do little more.

Those most involved can't simply walk away.
Their lives have changed forever from now on—
Those who remain defined by who is gone,
Those gone defined by who is forced to stay.

They greet the ones who come to say goodbye
And smile when all they want to do is cry.
Their well of anguish never can run dry,
Replenished by the next in line to die.

When death strikes down a stranger's soul, they care—
But empathy is more than they can bear.

Scars of Unrequited Love

The sting of loss crept back into my life
When I learned lately you had passed away.
Abandonment, forsaken vows, and strife
Destroyed the bond we had one yesterday.

I grieved your loss before, so long ago.
I felt I failed despite how hard I tried.
In moving on, I learned to heal and grow,
But wonder what you meant and when you lied.

The time we shared, it meant the world to me,
The promise we would make and you'd rescind,
It did not last and was not meant to be,
But know you were forgiven in the end.

I'm sorry that your life has ended thus
But grieve not like the day you ended us.

A Mended Heart

I sometimes think about what could have been,
Reflecting on my choices, big and small.
I wonder how I would improve it all
And what I'd change could life be lived again.

Could I have traveled on a different path?
Forgone the unrequited love and pain?
Have understood my loss was still my gain?
That love was waiting in the aftermath?

The golden bands on our left hands remind
This careworn soul that someone cared to stay.
The heartache was the price I had to pay,
To reach the point where our two paths entwined.

A mended heart is stronger in the end
Than one pristine which never had to mend.

The Captain to His Mate

These days I often pause to contemplate
How fortunate I am to share with you
Our struggles overcome which left our fate
Unbroken by the tempests rolling through.
God knows some days we've been denied a breeze;
However, we've survived the strongest gales
To right the ship and head for calmer seas,
Fair winds be damned as we unfurled the sails.
Until our voyage runs its natural course,
Land-sightings will be few and far between.
No hurricane nor like destructive force
Exists to make our journey less serene.
So long as you are with me on this trip,
Survival means I won't give up the ship.

Humilitas

There is this hope they will remember me,
While not with flags half-lowered on the pole,
As someone they would all aspire to be:
A model man—another kindred soul.

Intentions were befouled by circumstance.
Accomplishments seem slight when said aloud.
But when I failed to seize a second chance,
I still survived unbroken and unbowed.

There will be those who mark my death with tears
As substance passes quickly into shade;
I pray they judge my time productive years
And face their circumstances unafraid.

I leave this life to stand before a gate
And pray to God my name's upon the scroll,
That afterlife might grant a better fate
Than I deserve in judgments of the soul.

("Humilitas" shares the end word of each line with
William Ernest Henley's "Invictus.")

Echoes of Yesterday

She often sat here, decades long before
The writing there was added to the wall,
Wrapped snugly in her favorite knitted shawl,
Forgetting pains she'd chosen to ignore.

Her memory has faded like this chair—
Its finish chipped away; its cushions torn—
Few people now around were then to mourn,
And fewer still know who was sitting there.

It's easy to forget she settled here
And lived and worked with dreams of better days.
An optimist, she'd often count the ways
Tomorrow'd be the highlight of her year.

Yet now this soul has long returned to dust;
Possessions left to chip and fade and rust.

A Suitcase

A suitcase lies among the many things
Abandoned when the owner left for good.
Exposed to elements, old mildew clings
To fabric torn and peeling from the wood.

The dusty handle still emits a shine
In places that endured the frequent grasp
Of hands too hurried by the railroad line
To put on gloves or lock the metal clasp.

What irony! A suitcase left behind
Speaks more about the trip it never made,
Found useless for the task it was designed
When owner passed from substance into shade.

The things that matter now won't matter then.
The cycle only ends to start again.

Circus Elephants in Retirement

Does an elephant dream in his pachyderm dreams
Of the clowns and trapezes, the music, the shows?
Of a time in his prime which compared to now seems
Did encompass the best of the life that he knows?

Is she grateful to voices demanding the end
Of performances ladies and gentlemen share
As the best of events they were pleased to attend
Or resent being treated like some dancing bear?

Is retirement all it was promised to be?
Do they miss the excitement, the life on the train?
Would they choose to be loved rather than to be free?
Or perhaps they're content; free of stress; free of pain?

The Fall of the Fourth Estate

The Media: The Fourth Estate *
Performed disgracefully of late,
Delivering the news askew,
Allowing only viewpoints through
That fuel the discontent and hate.

Campaigning bullies will berate
The citizens and educate
Their friends to start deferring to
The Media.

All politicians propagate
Hypocrisy and subjugate
Constituents to their world view
While building up their revenue,
And few are eager to negate
The Media.

* "The Fourth Estate" is a term attributed to British politician Edmund Burke in 1787, referring to the press as a political force whose influence is not consistently or officially recognized.

Chaos Abounds

What thoughts are left unthought? What is profound?
Does any quest of value still remain?
So much that once was sacred, now profane,
Defines the soul still searching. Common ground
May not exist, but seldom is it sought.
Reflection rarely yields a different view.
Truth comes, it seems, in varied shade and hue,
And answers rarely mesh with what was taught.

Anarchy freely reigns; chaos abounds.
Conformity...coerced upon the few
By those expressing outrage, sure to sue
For feelings hurt on verbal battlegrounds.
So many taking action should refrain
From seeking pleasure in another's pain.

Made in China

"Made in China" reads the label—
Shattered on the coffee table:
Some cheap and broken plastic toys
We purchased for our girls and boys—

Imports purchased which enable
Labor camps that leave unstable
Lives in ruin and can disable
Limbs…but disregard the noise
Made in China.

Are our children really stable?
We disservice and mislabel
All the little girls and boys
Who grow up with cheap plastic toys;
Sold our souls and bought a fable
Made in China?

Indoctrinating Evil

A student sits and stares at an exam,
Expected there to demonstrate their hate.
But, something in their heart does not relate—
A pause before the slaughter of the lamb.

Could such a spark of conscience buried deep
Take root and cease the cycle of despair?
Can persecution—prevalence of terror—
Be stopped while making wolves out of the sheep?

The children taught to hate the Falun Gong
Continue dark and twisted legacies,
Creating needless animosities,
Divorced from rhyme and reason, right and wrong.

Indoctrinating children is the crime
Perpetuating evil over time.

Bad News

A glass of water, half consumed, remained
Neglected at the table where she sat
Before her father tenderly explained
How nothing can be done, and that is that.

Oh, how can one so quickly lose all hope?
She asked herself as numbness settled in.
And as she wondered how she'd ever cope
He thought about the places he had been,

The accolades he'd hung upon the wall
In black and silver frames, advanced degrees,
Group photos from his days of playing ball,
His membership in nine societies…

With all of these and more he was undone
By forces far outside of his control
Accomplishments, hard-earned, now felt unwon,
Despair crept in and grappled with his soul.

He'd trade it all if he could ease her pain.
He hadn't meant to make his daughter cry.
His life was lived too fully to complain,
Yet still he wasn't set to say goodbye.

They Boldly Went

They boldly went to outer space
To represent the human race
To aliens from far and wide
On planets unidentified—
Exotic and yet commonplace.

With others eager to debase
The Enterprise and to erase
Their dreams, both spoken and implied,
They boldly went.

Each journey to an unknown place
Brought challenges they had to face
Where differences were set aside,
Inspiring people nationwide.
And though some died, in every case
They boldly went.

What Will Stay?

Unyielding ancient Roman gods stare out
With sightless eyes on futures never seen,
The cold, dead stone contrasting with the green
Of life renewed and thriving all about.

Their likenesses, once known, are now obscure,
As will be those who we now cast in bronze.
Our kings and queens, our bishops, knights, and pawns,
Torn down by those who'll find our thoughts impure.

What will it matter, when we've gone away?
We primitive and unenlightened lot
Who've squandered time and grace so dearly bought,
What dear to us will fade, and what will stay?

They'll view us with a condescending air,
Interpreting what wasn't ever there.

Backwoods Town

The tattered glovebox map did not reflect
The backwards nature of this backwoods town.
I moved here to belong, instead I found
Contempt, which I did not at all expect.

My ancestors once lived here long ago;
The paper said they were respected then.
But no one living can remember when
They saw them here or who they used to know.

I'm cousins with a lot of those I met,
Though it seems not to matter that I'm kin.
I still am from the outside looking in:
Politeness and cold smiles are all I get.

That is, they smile until I turn my back.
And that is when they plan their next attack.

Physician of the Mind

This mannequin—lifeless, demure—
Will keep close secrets told secure,
Unlike that friend who in the end
Is quick to judge and less mature.

What troubles whispered through the years
Have bounced off these unhearing ears,
Unburdening a client's soul,
Absolving guilt, allaying fears?

This true physician of the mind,
Compassionate, unduly kind,
Is counselor, confessor, priest,
Conservator, and more—combined!

Blue Spacious Skies

Blue spacious skies meet greener pastures' hue,
Where sleepy woodland creatures rendezvous.
The fragrances of lilac and of fir
Are pungent in the air and would confer
A feeling of tranquility on you.

Your present rather dismal point of view
Is neither flexible nor even true.
You bring the rain; your outlook does defer
Blue spacious skies.

So, part the curtains wide; let sunshine through.
Find shooting stars at night with someone new.
Our lives go by in such a hasty blur.
You'll see things better than they ever were.
And cloudy days might suddenly incur
Blue spacious skies.

Depression's Lies

"Depression brings humility."
Her glaring inability?
Constructively self-criticize.
For criticizing amplifies
The flaws that only she can see.

Suppressing sensitivity
To camouflage fragility,
She flirts with failure if she tries.
"Depression brings humility."

Confronting fallibility,
Betrays innate servility,
If only she could realize
A way to stop believing lies;
Repeating in her mind, she cries:
"Depression brings humility."

An Affirmation of Faith?

The time I rolled my SUV
Forced me to face mortality.

As tires screeched, I lost control;
I barely stopped before a pole
But could have died there instantly.

My thoughts were hard to pigeonhole
And anxious feelings took their toll,
Reliving it inside my head—
How close I came to being dead
With each successive barrel roll.

No broken bones, I barely bled,
But life continued on instead.
The answer to another's prayer?
A blessing extraordinaire
Affirming faith for times ahead?

Encroaching Weeds

She'd not allow encroaching weeds
Among the flowers raised from seeds
In beds meticulously kept
Beyond the stable, neatly swept,
Across from where the light recedes.

But lately there've been other needs
Demanding time, and thus proceeds
Her garden to appear unkept.

She'd not allow her lesser breeds
To pair with her prize-winning steeds,
But in the dark and shadows crept
The vines and crab grass while she slept
Committing one of many deeds
She'd not allow.

The Edge of Memory

His laughter still infects across the years,
Long absent since the days he was around—
The video conserves the cherished sound—
Distorted by effects of time and tears.

He occupies the edge of memory.
His ghost still haunts me when I least expect.
Yet, when I pause and try to recollect,
He hides in haze devoid of clarity.

So different than the person in my mind,
The one who now appears upon the screen
Objectively preserved, but seldom seen,
Is more authentic and far less refined.

I cannot trust my head to hold what's dear;
My heart and time are sure to interfere.

On Better Days

On better days, the scented summer air
Would softly blow and gently tease my hair;
Few news events gave rise to much alarm;
We never felt we'd come to any harm;
The world had problems, but we didn't care.

But now we're told we always must prepare
For darker times ahead. The headlines scare
More than inform—incite more than disarm.

On better days,
My thoughts return more frequently to where
An optimistic child once played, and there
On summer days exploring grandpa's farm,
The future's possibilities had charm,
And we had positivity to spare...
On better days.

Reflection

I watched him slowly growing old and frail
But still he passed before I was prepared—
A dreadful fight in which few men prevail
Approached with peace where others have despaired.

I often try in vain to recollect
The many times he spoke my name with pride,
Occasionally pausing to reflect
On memories less stark than when he died.

Now when I stare into a looking glass,
I see his features blended in my own
And shed a tear despite the years that pass—
A kinder, wiser man I've never known.

I only hope when someone measures me,
I'm half the man he showed me how to be.

Out of Mind

Dark images my memory retains:
A dying loved one's final, raspy breath,
The empty stare, the gaping maw of death,
Contrasting what was lost with what remains.

Forgetting what the coffin, closed, contains,
Most soldier on, neglecting fragile health,
Resume their focus on amassing wealth
Until the blood stops flowing through their veins.

But what's another cautionary tale?
Didactic, preachy warnings from the grave,
Inadequate to teach, much less to save,
Ensure that fools continue to prevail
In wasting time regardless of the cost
And finding out too late what has been lost.

Blades of Doubt

There may be greater horrors for causing dread
Than chinks within the armor of the mind
Where blades of doubt impale the hope they find
One holds for not communing with the dead.

Worms feast upon the flesh of those who fed
Upon the myths of immortality—
Not speaking of religiosity,
But time extended here on Earth instead.

There must be more than limiting one's fear
In seeking resurrection for the soul—
A humbler and far more modest goal
Than dodging death, but never less sincere.

Pursuits which mark our struggle for control
Intensify as chaos gathers near.

The Air Grows Cold

The air grows cold. The leaves, once green,
Turn yellow, orange, and gold between
Long hours spent indoors. The call
Of birds of prey make forests crawl
With anxious creatures seldom seen.

Close by, as in some magazine,
A brook completes the perfect scene.
As humid summer yields to fall,
The air grows cold.

Soon winter comes: first Halloween,
Then heaters run on kerosene,
A knitted scarf and hat, a shawl,
But well before the snow and all,
The air grows cold.

While Waiting

While waiting for the Greyhound bus,
My dad and I, the two of us,
Recounted pleasant moments passed:
The memories we had amassed,
Experienced, and oft discussed.

Our dialog continued thus—
Light-hearted and extraneous—
Until we saw the bus at last
While waiting.

We said goodbye without much fuss;
I stepped into the ominous,
Uncharted future from the past
Not knowing how my die was cast
And feeling I grew up too fast
While waiting.

Forgotten

The grass has overgrown the weathered stone
Since they first placed his body in the ground,
And visitors no longer come around
With hope they'll not, in turn, face death alone.

Did Life, for him, contrast this sorry end?
You'd never know by glancing at the name.
In fact, all resting places look the same—
A fate we'll meet but never comprehend.

Once fragile flesh and memories decay,
The brush grows thick, and ivy starts to climb.
The lichen steals identities with time.
Precipitation wears the stone away.

Few living souls know whose remains are there;
Not even their descendants really care.

About the Author

Randal A. Burd, Jr. has been writing poetry for publication since middle school, when a silly poem he wrote in the fifth grade (1989), "I Have a Hippoturtlephant," was published by *Creative Kids* magazine. His poetry continues to be featured in numerous literary journals, both online and in print.

Randal holds a bachelor's degree in English Literature from Missouri University of Science & Technology where he was Editor-in-Chief of both the college newspaper and the literary magazine for multiple terms. He also holds a master's degree in English Curriculum & Instruction from the University of Missouri.

Randal is currently the Editor-in-Chief of the online literary magazine *Sparks of Calliope.* He has also been heard occasionally on Poetry Super Highway's monthly Worldwide Open Poetry Reading. Randal is a married father of two and educator teaching disadvantaged youth and adults in rural Missouri.

Made in the USA
Columbia, SC
08 September 2020